ANTIDOTES

INFORMATION AND AMMUNITION TO GET YOU
THROUGH YOUR DAY IN SALES AND SALES
MANAGEMENT FROM A
REAL DOOR-TO-DOOR SALESMAN

BY

THE GENERAL

Bloomington, IN   Milton Keynes, UK
authorHOUSE®

AuthorHouse™
1663 Liberty Drive, Suite 200
Bloomington, IN 47403
www.authorhouse.com
Phone: 1-800-839-8640

AuthorHouse™ UK Ltd.
500 Avebury Boulevard
Central Milton Keynes, MK9 2BE
www.authorhouse.co.uk
Phone: 08001974150

First published by AuthorHouse 3/6/2007

Printed in the United States of America
Bloomington, Indiana

This book is printed on acid-free paper.

ISBN: 978-1-4259-9281-1 (sc)
ISBN: 978-1-4259-9280-4 (hc)

Library of Congress Control Number: 2007901171

Forward by David Kayne:

I first met "The General" when I was recruited into direct sales. He was still in his early twenties and was a recruiter for our company. He pulled up in a new Corvette, wore expensive suits and a Rolex watch. I thought, let's see what this guy is all about. I had heard that he did a nice job helping companies get turned around with their recruiting and training of salespeople.

When I opened my first business, I had The General come in to help. He helped me qualify and earn my own franchise with my company. I quickly relocated out of state to a bigger market and contacted him to help me once again get established. It was difficult at first, but my wife, Tracy, and I were fortunate through our hard work. We prospered and grew our business into several successful companies. The General and I stayed close friends and our friendship grew. Now, twenty years later with nothing to prove, I wanted to make another good run with one of my companies. I had The General come in again. This time I gave him carte blanche. The result? He inspired my existing people to new heights and recruited some great new salespeople who enabled my business to set a new record. We became one of the most valuable and top franchises in the world today.

You see, I know The General personally after twenty years of working with him. I am also the one who gave him his name— "The General."

I hope that you enjoy the book and the philosophy in it. Over the years, I have witnessed firsthand how many people have prospered and grown to new heights by implementing the basic fundamentals of salesmanship and management The General talks about in his book.

Enjoy,

David Kayne

PERSONAL
SELLING

Tips from The General on the sales business…

I've always tried to go one step past what everyone else expected of me in the sales business. People sure remember your name then.

Got it? Now go to work…

~The General

How this impacted my day:

When you go one step ahead what everyone does it is to be better and be remembered & recognize. Which is the main reason I work so hard is to be known as the best or on my way to being one of the best.

Tips from The General on the sales business…

Nobody in sales will believe you unless you believe in yourself.

Got it? Now go to work…

~The General

How this impacted my day:

When you believe in yourself it
gives you the confidence to know
that what-ever obstacle you go
threw at work you will get threw
it cause you can't fool yourself.

Tips from The General on the sales business…

Only you can be yourself. No one else is qualified for the job.

Got it? Now go to work…

       ~The General

How this impacted my day:

Be yourself when you are
being watch and when your
not Because who you are
when no one is watching is
who you really are. Be that
person all the time.

Tips from The General on the sales business...

After you have tried everything else you have thought of on your own to do, sometimes you just have to take the medicine and do it the way you are supposed to do it.

Got it? Now go to work...

~The General

How this impacted my day:

When it comes to work to me this means just following the program because what you know in this business to do won't make you successfull it what you suppose to do that will get you where you have to go. Just do what you know you suppose to and success will follow

7

Tips from The General on the sales business…

Oftentimes in sales, you run into associates who don't know what they want from their career but are willing to go through hell to get it. Find out what you want—fast!

Got it? Now go to work…

~The General

How this impacted my day:

If you know what you want you work towards it. Work for something & keeping goals in mind makes you better if you don't have goals you stay in one place and don't grow! You SHOULD BE GROWING IN YOUR CAREER Everyday!

Tips from The General on the sales business…

A big shot is simply a little shot that kept on shooting…

Zig Ziglar

Got it? Now go to work…

~The General

How this impacted my day:

If you don't make the shot the first time keep trying. Not giving up is the key.

Tips from The General on the sales business…

First, you must visualize the kind of person you want to be in your business. Sound silly? Not as silly as the position you're in right now. Try it. It works!

Got it? Now go to work…

~The General

How this impacted my day:

If I see myself as a DT Know, when I get there the, Job won't be, that hard cause, I would have had a lot of training by careing myself in that matter.

Tips from The General on the sales business…

If you spend fifteen minutes a day learning something new about your business, in no time you will be an expert at it. Imagine your income level at something you are an expert at!

Got it? Now go to work…

~The General

How this impacted my day:

Experts at anything get paid top dollars and that's the reason we all work for maximum income so become an expert at what you do fast and the expert money will follow suit.

Tips from The General on the sales business…

If I had a formula for bypassing trouble, I wouldn't pass it around. Wouldn't be doing anyone a favor. Trouble creates a capacity to handle it.

> *Oliver Wendell Holmes*

Got it? Now go to work…

> *~The General*

How this impacted my day:

How we handle our troubles show our character. By handling your troubles it makes your stronger for the next obstical that you will have to go through next. Capacity to handle troubles keep you going day by day.

Tips from The General on the sales business…

You'd better start getting interested in your future now. That's where you're going to spend the rest of your life.

Got it? Now go to work…

~The General

How this impacted my day:

Even if you don't get interested in your
future your still gonna spend the rest
of your there so why not get interested
in it so that it is somewhere you
wanna be when you get there.

Tips from The General on the sales business…

Activity is contagious. Get active today and you will get the results that you want.

Got it? Now go to work…

                                  ~The General

How this impacted my day:

Hard work pays off!!! You can't expect to not be active and get the same results as being fully active in what your doing. Also when others see the results from your effort they will want to do the same

Tips from The General on the sales business…

Most of your "first time things in life" scared you. That means they were worth it. Make this first time in sales the last career you will ever need.

Got it? Now go to work…

~The General

How this impacted my day:

Make your career in sales worth it. especially if its your first time in the sales business.

Tips from The General on the sales business…

A positive attitude is great, but to move to the next level, you also need positive action.

Got it? Now go to work…

~The General

How this impacted my day:

Positive action equals positive results
Its not what you can say. Its all
about what you can do.

Tips from The General on the sales business…

Raise your personal standards and watch it turn to consistency.

Got it? Now go to work…

~The General

How this impacted my day:

If you continue to raise your standards your results will never be less ~~than~~ ~~short~~ You may fall a bit short but it would be better to fall short than to fall flat. And you'll continue to push push, push.

Tips from The General on the sales business…

Mark my words, you lie down with dogs and you will wake up with fleas…

Got it? Now go to work…

~The General

How this impacted my day:

Watch the company that you keep!.
Whatever attitude they have oan
be transported to you whether
you want it to or not.

02/14/08

Tips from The General on the sales business…

Your energy level will always go where your focus is.

Got it? Now go to work…

                              ~The General

How this impacted my day:

what ever your trully focus on
is where your gonna put all you
energy cause you wantha be
great at your main focus.

                                        02/15

Tips from The General on the sales business…

Start your day with these four questions. You will make every day a more productive one.

1. **What is the best thing that can happen to me today?**
2. **What is the worst thing that can happen to me today?**
3. **What can I do to make sure the best thing does happen to me today?**
4. **What can I do to make sure the worst thing does not happen to me today?**

Got it? Now go to work…

~The General

How this impacted my day:

Stay positive and do what you have to do to keep your day as positive as it can be.

02/16

Tips from The General on the sales business…

Challenges in sales? Every day. They are stepping stones or stumbling blocks. How do you view them?

Got it? Now go to work…

~The General

How this impacted my day:

I view challenges in sales as stepping stones because when they come up I do whatever I can to overcome them to keep rising to the top challenges gives you something to over come and get better at. 02/17

Tips from The General on the sales business…

I am only one, but I am still one. I cannot do everything, but I can still do something; I will not refuse to do something I can do.

Helen Keller

Got it? Now go to work…

~The General

How this impacted my day:

I am my own entity, and I am a force. I may be only one but I also can get the job done. I don't have to be afraid to do something that looks hard cause its only me.
I AM!!!   02/18

Tips from The General on the sales business…

Never expect a negative attitude in sales to give you positive results.

Got it? Now go to work…

~The General

How this impacted my day:

_____
_____
_____
_____
_____
_____

Tips from The General on the sales business…

There are three types of people in sales—those who make it happen, those who watch it happen, and those who wonder what happened. Which one are you?

Got it? Now go to work…

~The General

How this impacted my day:

_____
_____
_____
_____
_____
_____

Tips from The General on the sales business…

People are not sales resistant, they are salespeople resistant. Nobody likes to be sold but everyone loves to buy. Learn the difference and you will sell more product.

Got it? Now go to work…

~The General

How this impacted my day:

Tips from The General on the sales business…

A positive attitude is contagious. Be a carrier.

Got it? Now go to work…

~The General

How this impacted my day:

_____
_____
_____
_____
_____
_____

Tips from The General on the sales business…

A turtle only makes progress when it sticks its neck out. Stick your neck out on some things you have never done before today.

Got it? Now go to work…

~The General

How this impacted my day:

_____
_____
_____
_____
_____
_____

Tips from The General on the sales business...

Knocked on twenty-five doors and still can't get a presentation? Knock on twenty-six.

Got it? Now go to work...

~The General

How this impacted my day:

_____
_____
_____
_____
_____
_____

Tips from The General on the sales business...

When asked what he thought about when he struck out, Babe Ruth said, "I think about hitting home runs." Relate that to your sales career.

Got it? Now go to work...

~The General

How this impacted my day:

Tips from The General on the sales business...

You want success in sales? Here are four sure fire rules for it:

1. *Show up.*
2. *Pay attention.*
3. *Ask questions.*
4. *Don't quit.*

Got it? Now go to work...

~The General

How this impacted my day:

Tips from The General on the sales business…

My old bulldog's nose was inverted. That was so he could still breathe while biting down in a fight. Sometimes your career will be a fight. Remember this…never, never, never, never, never give up! Never!

Got it? Now go to work…

~The General

How this impacted my day:

_____
_____
_____
_____
_____
_____

Tips from The General on the sales business…

I have never seen a monument erected to a pessimist.

Paul Harvey

Got it? Now go to work…

~The General

How this impacted my day:

_____
_____
_____
_____
_____
_____

Tips from The General on the sales business...

Success in sales seems to be largely a matter of hanging on after others have let go. Are you the last one out of your hiring class?

Got it? Now go to work...

~The General

How this impacted my day:

Tips from The General on the sales business...

It takes many blows to drive a nail in the dark; so unnecessary. Get yourself educated in your business and the lights will come on. Your job titles will change faster on your business cards than you can imagine.

Got it? Now go to work...

~The General

How this impacted my day:

Tips from The General on the sales business...

It is not the smartest or the strongest who make it in sales. It's the ones who are the most responsive to changes. Changes will happen with your product, management, financing and company. Roll with it.

Got it? Now go to work...

~The General

How this impacted my day:

_____
_____
_____
_____
_____
_____

Tips from The General on the sales business...

Get wise in the sales business and move up before you get old in the sales business.

Got it? Now go to work...

~The General

How this impacted my day:

_____
_____
_____
_____
_____
_____

Tips from The General on the sales business…

It's easy to accept that the dream is over in sales. Keep pushing, and it will soon be well worth it.

Got it? Now go to work…

~The General

How this impacted my day:

Tips from The General on the sales business…

Success in sales is a choice. Use it or lose it.

Got it? Now go to work…

~The General

How this impacted my day:

_____
_____
_____
_____
_____
_____

Tips from The General on the sales business...

You will never know what is possible in your sales career until you set a goal to do it.

Got it? Now go to work...

~The General

How this impacted my day:

Tips from The General on the sales business...

Blah, blah, blah, blah, blah. Quit talking about doing it, and go sell some product now.

Got it? Now go to work...

~The General

How this impacted my day:

Tips from The General on the sales business...

It's never too late to be the person you want to be in your sales company.

Got it? Now go to work...

~The General

How this impacted my day:

Tips from The General on the sales business…

Keep away from people who belittle your ambitions. Small people can always do that, but the really great ones make you feel that you, too, can become great.

Mark Twain

Got it? Now go to work…

~The General

How this impacted my day:

_____
_____
_____
_____
_____
_____

Tips from The General on the sales business…

If you do not stretch yourself in your sales career or your personal life, God will come in and do things to make you stretch. Sometimes you won't like the things that will happen then.

Got it? Now go to work…

~The General

How this impacted my day:

_____
_____
_____
_____
_____
_____

Tips from The General on the sales business...

Where do you see yourself in five years with your sales career?

Got it? Now go to work...

~The General

How this impacted my day:

Tips from The General on the sales business...

Nothing is easy to the unwilling in sales.

Got it? Now go to work...

~The General

How this impacted my day:

_____
_____
_____
_____
_____
_____

Tips from The General on the sales business…

Become flexible in sales. You will never get bent out of shape.

Got it? Now go to work…

~The General

How this impacted my day:

_____

Tips from The General on the sales business…

If we all did what we are capable of doing in our business, we would shock ourselves.

Got it? Now go to work…

~The General

How this impacted my day:

_____

_____

_____

_____

_____

_____

Tips from The General on the sales business…

Success isn't permanent and failure isn't fatal.

Coach Mike Ditka

Got it? Now go to work…

~The General

How this impacted my day:

_____
_____
_____
_____
_____
_____

Tips from The General on the sales business…

Change your thoughts about your sales career and it will change your world in your sales career.

Got it? Now go to work…

~The General

How this impacted my day:

_____

_____

_____

_____

_____

_____

Tips from The General on the sales business…

Personality can open doors for product presentations. Excitement in that presentation keeps you in the presentation. Get excited today!

Got it? Now go to work…

~The General

How this impacted my day:

_____
_____
_____
_____
_____
_____

Tips from The General in the sales business...

*Money is not the most important thing in sales.
Love is. Fortunately, we love money. It's up there,
close to air and oxygen on the must-have list.*

Got it? Now go to work...

~The General

How this impacted my day:

Tips from The General on the sales business...

You can fail many times in your sales career, but you're not a failure until you start blaming someone else for your failures.

Got it? Now go to work...

~The General

How this impacted my day:

Tips from The General on the sales business…

The opportunity to sell your product presents itself every time you meet someone. Be ready for the opportunity and talk up your business. You will get one or two more this month when you do this.

Got it? Now go to work…

~The General

How this impacted my day:

_____

_____

_____

_____

_____

_____

Tips from The General on the sales business...

Your career in sales will be like riding an escalator. You can ride it up for fortune or ride it down for misery. Never will you stand still.

Got it? Now go to work...

~The General

How this impacted my day:

_____
_____
_____
_____
_____
_____

Tips from The General on the sales business…

Okay, you learned something new today, big deal. It's worthless unless you take action on it.

Got it? Now go to work…

~The General

How this impacted my day:

_____
_____
_____
_____
_____
_____

Tips from The General on the sales business...

Quit finding things to amuse yourself with all day and go sell some product.

Got it? Now go to work...

~The General

How this impacted my day:

Tips from The General on the sales business…

Keep telling yourself you're not a failure. You just failed at trying to do something. Another thing… they're not saying no to you, just your offer to them.

Got it? Now go to work…

~The General

How this impacted my day:

_____

_____

_____

_____

_____

_____

Tips from The General on the sales business...

The hardest thing about making commitments is following through with them.

Got it? Now go to work...

~The General

How this impacted my day:

Tips from The General on the sales business…

Stop doing what you know does not work in your sales career.

Got it? Now go to work…

~The General

How this impacted my day:

_____

_____

_____

_____

_____

_____

Tips from

Confiden　　　　　　　　　　　*ır*
product. (　　　　　　　　　　*duct.*

Got it? N

　　　　　　　　　　　　　　　.neral

How this impacted my day:

_____
_____
_____
_____
_____
_____

Tips from The General on the sales business...

Just "go long today" and "swing for the fences."
Inspire yourself and others along the way.

Got it? Now go to work...

~The General

How this impacted my day:

Tips from The General on the sales business…

Fortune is <u>always</u> on the side of the strong. Get strong in your sales career and watch yourself make a fortune.

Got it? Now go to work…

~The General

How this impacted my day:

_____
_____
_____
_____
_____
_____

Tips from The General on the sales business...

The absolute worst thing that can happen to you is that they so "no" to you today. Can you handle that?

Got it? Now go to work...

~The General

How this impacted my day:

_____
_____
_____
_____
_____
_____

Tips from The General in the sales business…

What goes around comes around—but never in time for when you need it. Don't wait for things to happen to you. Make things happen.

Got it? Now go to work…

~The General

How this impacted my day:

Tips from The General on the sales business...

Become "sales-tough" as quickly as possible. You will know when you have.

Got it? Now go to work...

~The General

How this impacted my day:

Tips from The General on the sales business…

Many words said; many lies said. That is how most customers think. Watch how much you talk and K.I.S.S.

Got it? Now go to work…

~The General

How this impacted my day:

Tips from The General on the sales business…

Money earned as commission is twice as sweet as money given to us by salary.

Got it? Now go to work…

~The General

How this impacted my day:

_____
_____
_____
_____
_____
_____

Tips from The General in the sales business…

Stick to what you know is best in your sales career and your company. Trees often planted in the yards of mansions seldom prosper. Stay with your company and excel if you can.

Got it? Now go to work…

~The General

How this impacted my day:

_____

_____

_____

_____

_____

_____

Tips from the General on the sales business…

No customer's credit is as good as their cash. Focus on getting the cash today.

Got it? Now go to work…

~The General

How this impacted my day:

Tips from The General on the sales business…

Teach yourself to say, "I don't know" until you do know. It sure saves a lot of time and saves you plenty of sales when you are new.

Got it? Now go to work…

~The General

How this impacted my day:

Tips from The General on the sales business…

Even a mouse keeps three holes. Find three ways of making money with your company.

Got it? Now go to work…

~The General

How this impacted my day:

Tips from The General on the sales business...

Promise little on your sales, and then deliver much to them.

Got it? Now go to work...

~The General

How this impacted my day:

Tips from The General on the sales business…

Denial is not a river in Egypt. Denial is ignoring the obvious.

Zig Ziglar

Got it? Now go to work…

~The General

How this impacted my day:

_____
_____
_____
_____
_____
_____

Tips from The General on the sales business...

Teach your mind to growl like your stomach when it is hungry for knowledge.

Got it? Now go to work...

~The General

How this impacted my day:

Tips from The General on the sales business...

Boldness in sales is your first priority—and the second—and the third.

Got it? Now go to work...

~The General

How this impacted my day:

Tips from The General on the sales business...

You want safety, security and three meals a day? Go to prison. Don't like that idea? Become a student of your business and succeed. Others have done it, and so can you.

Got it? Now go to work...

~The General

How this impacted my day:

_____
_____
_____
_____
_____
_____

Tips from The General on the sales business...

Coffee is for closers...

> *Alec Baldwin – Actor*
> *Glenn Gary – Glenn Ross*

Got it? Now go to work...

> *~The General*

How this impacted my day:

_____
_____
_____
_____
_____
_____

Tips from The General on the sales business…

When you get bored with what you are doing, you become a real pain. Get fired up!

Got it? Now go to work…

~The General

How this impacted my day:

_____
_____
_____
_____
_____
_____

Tips from The General on the sales business…

The wishbone will never replace the backbone.

Got it? Now go to work…

~The General

How this impacted my day:

_____
_____
_____
_____
_____
_____

Tips from The General on the sales business…

211 degrees is hot; 212 degrees is boiling. Only one degree makes all the difference. Turn it up a few degrees today and see what happens.

Got it? Now go to work…

~The General

How this impacted my day:

Tips from The General on the sales business…

Proper direction sure saves a ton of time in the sales business. Carpenters always measure twice and cut once. Get better on your direction today.

Got it? Now go to work…

~The General

How this impacted my day:

Tips from The General on the sales business...

Either you work towards your own personal goals or you are helping someone else reach their own personal goals. The choice is yours.

Got it? Now go to work...

~The General

How this impacted my day:

Tips from The General on the sales business…

Try this one today … Do "extreme selling."
You figure it out.

Got it? Now go to work…

~The General

How this impacted my day:

Tips from The General on the sales business...

People who show their true good character daily will always succeed unless they quit.

Got it? Now go to work...

~The General

How this impacted my day:

_____
_____
_____
_____
_____
_____

Tips from The General on the sales business…

If you can't tell your manager about it… you really should not be doing it.

Got it? Now go to work…

~The General

How this impacted my day:

Tips from The General on the sales business…

Programs do not fail … people do.

Got it? Now go to work…

~The General

How this impacted my day:

Tips from The General on the sales business..

A goal is simply your dreams with a deadline. Set some new goals today.

Got it? Now go to work...

~The General

How this impacted my day:

_____

_____

_____

_____

_____

_____

Tips from The General on the sales business...

Make failure your teacher, not your undertaker.

Zig Ziglar

Got it? Now go to work...

~The General

How this impacted my day:

_____

_____

_____

_____

_____

_____

Tips from The General on the sales business…

Do you want to be a champion? You only have to work half-days to be successful—the first twelve hours or the second twelve hours.

Got it? Now go to work…

~The General

How this impacted my day:

Tips from The General on the sales business…

You will never know what is possible until you set a goal to do it. Stop saying you're going to do it and just do it today—right now!

Got it? Now go to work…

~The General

How this impacted my day:

Tips from The General on the sales business…

Success is largely due to how good you are and how many people you talk to daily.

Got it? Now go to work…

~The General

How this impacted my day:

Tips from The General on the sales business...

Rapport—the magic ingredient. Find commonalities with your prospects. It will ignite and energize them to open up to you. Their checkbooks will open soon after.

Got it? Now go to work...

~The General

How this impacted my day:

_____
_____
_____
_____
_____
_____

Tips from The General on the sales business...

Pessimistic people are just afraid of failure.

Got it? Now go to work...

~The General

How this impacted my day:

Tips from The General on the sales business...

Stop doing what you know does not work. You're starting to look ridiculous now.

Got it? Now go to work...

~The General

How this impacted my day:

Tips from The General on the sales business…

Minds are like parachutes—they function only when open.

Thomas Dewar

Got it? Now go to work…

~The General

How this impacted my day:

_____
_____
_____
_____
_____
_____

Tips from The General on the sales business...

If you want something you've never had, you have to do something you've never done. If you want to do something you've never done, you have to become someone you've never been. That means you must change. Grow and get out of your comfort zone.

Got it? Now go to work...

~The General

How this impacted my day:

Tips from The General on the sales business...

Stop wishing things will change. Accept the fact that you are not getting the results you want. Get honest with yourself and get your problems solved.

Got it? Now go to work...

~The General

How this impacted my day:

_____
_____
_____
_____
_____
_____

Tips from The General on the sales business…

Today's prospects. No problem…
- *Prepare yourself.*
- *Make a great first impression.*
- *Find out how your goods or services will benefit them.*
- *Give 100% in your presentation.*

Got it? Now go to work…

~The General

How this impacted my day:

Tips from The General on the sales business…

Most of my successes came when I hustled.
Understand this—it doesn't take talent to hustle.
Just the will to do it.

Got it? Now go to work…

~The General

How this impacted my day:

_____
_____
_____
_____
_____
_____

Tips from The General on the sales business...

Nothing carries more weight or influence around your company or business like being a good example. Be a good soldier and a strong example. They will beg you to take on a promotion then.

Got it? Now go to work...

~The General

How this impacted my day:

_____
_____
_____
_____
_____
_____

Tips from The General on the sales business…

Thoughts become actions; actions become habits; habits become character; character becomes your destiny.

~Unknown

Got it? Now go to work…

~The General

How this impacted my day:

Tips from The General on the sales business…

Success doesn't discriminate. It is an equal opportunity employer. It is available to everyone willing to pay the price.

Got it? Now go to work…

~The General

How this impacted my day:

_____
_____
_____
_____
_____
_____

Tips from The General on the sales business...

Good salespeople look for opportunities. When they don't find one, they create them.

Got it? Now go to work...

                              ~The General

How this impacted my day:

Tips from The General on the sales business…

Dream big dreams. Try cramming a great life into your tiny dreams.

Got it? Now go to work…

~The General

How this impacted my day:

\---
\---
\---
\---
\---
\---

Tips from The General on the sales business...

The experts in your business were once beginners in your business. Never forget that.

Got it? Now go to work...

~The General

How this impacted my day:

_____
_____
_____
_____
_____
_____

Tips from The General on the sales business...

Almost daily, you will run into people who tell you that your dreams are too big and your goals are unattainable. Walk away from them.

Got it? Now go to work...

~The General

How this impacted my day:

_____
_____
_____
_____
_____
_____

Tips from The General on the sales business...

Good salespeople do what bad salespeople are just too lazy to do in most cases. Catch yourself getting lazy before someone else catches you.

Got it? Now go to work...

~The General

How this impacted my day:

\---

\---

\---

\---

\---

\---

Tips from The General on the sales business…

The road to success in the sales business is unfortunately a toll road.

Got it? Now go to work…

~The General

How this impacted my day:

Tips from The General on the sales business...

Stop giving a mediocre presentation. You're never going to get better or get promoted that way and you're starting to look ridiculous.

Got it? Now go to work...

~The General

How this impacted my day:

_____

_____

_____

_____

_____

_____

Tips from The General on the sales business...

Show me a successful salesperson and I will show you a person who knows and understands sacrifice.

Got it? Now go to work...

~The General

How this impacted my day:

_____

_____

_____

_____

_____

_____

Tips from The General on the sales business...

Every day, fight the urge to be average. Average is the best of the worst, or the worst of the best. It's no place I ever want to be.

Got it? Now go to work...

                                        ~The General

How this impacted my day:

_____
_____
_____
_____
_____
_____

Tips from The General on the sales business...

The sales business doesn't require that we be the very best—only that you try to be your very best.

Got it? Now go to work...

~The General

How this impacted my day:

_____
_____
_____
_____
_____
_____

Tips from The General on the sales business…

You chose to be in sales. Now take it to the next level.

Got it? Now go to work…

~The General

How this impacted my day:

_____
_____
_____
_____
_____
_____

Tips from The General on the sales business…

Nothing ruins the truth in your presentation like s-t-r-e-t-c-h-ing it. Don't do it and please don't start it. You won't sell anymore, and in the long run, you will sell less.

Got it? Now go to work…

~The General

How this impacted my day:

_____
_____
_____
_____
_____
_____

Tips from The General on the sales business...

Triumph is just "umph" added to try.

Got it? Now go to work...

~The General

How this impacted my day:

_____
_____
_____
_____
_____
_____

Tips from The General on the sales business...

Feed your faith about what you do for a living and you will starve your doubts to death.

Got it? Now go to work...

~The General

How this impacted my day:

Tips from The General on the sales business...

If the going gets easy, you're probably going downhill.

Got it? Now go to work...

~The General

How this impacted my day:

Tips from The General on the sales business...

It is almost impossible to beat a person who doesn't give up. Be the person who doesn't give up.

Got it? Now go to work...

~The General

How this impacted my day:

Tips from The General on the sales business...

Make really good friends in the sales business long before you need them.

P.S. You will need them one day.

Got it? Now go to work...

                                        ~The General

How this impacted my day:

_____
_____
_____
_____
_____
_____

Tips from The General on the sales business…

Of all the things you wear to work everyday, your smile is the most important. Also, look people in the eye more when you talk with them. These are just a few of the things keeping you from being really great.

Got it? Now go to work…

~The General

How this impacted my day:

_____
_____
_____
_____
_____
_____

Tips from The General on the sales business...

Swallowing your pride does not lead to indigestion. If you're having trouble with something, get some help...NOW!

Got it? Now go to work...

~The General

How this impacted my day:

Tips from The General on the sales business...

Your future in the sales business is purchased by what you are doing in the present.

Got it? Now go to work...

~The General

How this impacted my day:

\---
\---
\---
\---
\---
\---

Tips from The General on the sales business...

You have all these great ideas... They won't work unless YOU DO.

Got it? Now go to work...

~The General

How this impacted my day:

Tips from The General on the sales business…

Procrastination is the assassination of motivation.

Got it? Now go to work…

~The General

How this impacted my day:

_____
_____
_____
_____
_____
_____

Tips from The General on the sales business...

Whenever you give someone one of your prospects whom you did not want, they always sell it.

Got it? Now go to work...

~The General

How this impacted my day:

Tips from The General on the sales business...

Being late for an appointment is a whole lot better than a $100.00 speeding ticket.

Got it? Now go to work...

                                        ~The General

How this impacted my day:

Tips from The General on the sales business…

The next move in sales is yours…

Got it? Now go to work…

~The General

How this impacted my day:

LEADERSHIP

&

MANAGEMENT

Tips from The General on the sales management part of the business...

If your character was "for sale," would it go for a discount or at full price?

Got it? Now go to work...

~The General

How this impacted my day:

_____
_____
_____
_____
_____
_____

Tips from The General on the sales management part of the business…

What your people talk about "by themselves" is the culture of what is happening in your organization or team.

Got it? Now go to work…

~The General

How this impacted my day:

Tips from The General on the sales management part of the business...

Stop pre-judging new recruits. I have seen many pull up on bicycles when they started. We get them through the program and they now drive a new Mercedes. Get better at this one.

Got it? Now go to work...

~The General

How this impacted my day:

_____
_____
_____
_____
_____
_____

Tips from The General on the sales management part of the business...

You must be willing to lose a good person or a sale to uphold the structure of your company or area of responsibility.

> *David Kayne*
> *Business owner*

Got it? Now go to work...

> *~The General*

How this impacted my day:

_____
_____
_____
_____
_____
_____

Tips from The General on the sales management part of the business…

Get "uncomfortable" again. Your business or area of responsibility will take off again. You know this is true. Be willing to do it again.

Got it? Now go to work…

                                        ~The General

How this impacted my day:

_____
_____
_____
_____
_____
_____

Tips from The General on the sales management part of the business…

Give your salespeople a deadline—sixty days to learn to sell. After that, they need to learn how to teach. Your business will take off after that.

Got it? Now go to work…

~The General

How this impacted my day:

Tips from The General on the sales management part of the business...

Submit yourself to authority and follow your company's programs. Your home office will be shocked and do more things for you than they ever did before. By the way, your business will increase also.

Got it? Now go to work...

~The General

How this impacted my day:

_____

_____

_____

_____

_____

_____

Tips from The General on the sales management part of the business...

If you can think it, you can ink it.

Got it? Now go to work...

~The General

How this impacted my day:

Tips from The General on the sales management part of the business...

Most managers don't know they actually have two products...the first is what you are selling. The second is the opportunity for them. Get good at selling both of them today.

Got it? Now go to work...

~The General

How this impacted my day:

_____
_____
_____
_____
_____
_____

Tips from the General on the sales management part of the business…

Can't decide on a new tattoo? Try this one:

"Recruit-Train-Develop-Promote."

Got it? Now go to work…

~The General

How this impacted my day:

_____

_____

_____

_____

_____

_____

Tips from The General on the sales management part of the business...

Most people hate bosses—that's understandable. Don't be a boss then. People want a leader, and they want a hero whom they can follow. Stop managing and start leading.

Got it? Now go to work...

~The General

How this impacted my day:

_____
_____
_____
_____
_____
_____

Tips from The General on the sales management part of the business...

Sometimes you have to punish one in an effort to teach the others...

Got it? Now go to work...

~The General

How this impacted my day:

Tips from The General on the sales management part of the business...

You lose rights every time you get a promotion.

- *You lost the right to talk or be negative.*
- *You lost the right to be late.*
- *You lost the right to not lead by example.*
- *You lost the right to not look your best everyday.*
- *You are no longer "one of the boys."*
- *You can no longer blame people.*

You will always retain the right to ask for help and advice though.

Got it? Now go to work...

~The General

How this impacted my day:

Tips from The General on the sales management part of the business...

As a manager, you will never know your people's characters until you have helped them get a client, close the deal, give them the credit and the entire commission for it.

Got it? Now go to work...

~The General

How this impacted my day:

_____
_____
_____
_____
_____
_____

Tips from The General on the sales management part of the business...

Hold yourself responsible for a higher standard than people expect of you in your company. Never excuse yourself.

Got it? Now go to work...

~The General

How this impacted my day:

Tips from The General on the sales management part of the business...

You can multiply your success in sales by dividing it. Go develop some superstars today.

Got it? Now go to work...

~The General

How this impacted my day:

Tips from The General on the sales management part of the business…

I would rather have 1% of 100 men's efforts than 100% of my own efforts.

Henry Ford

Got it? Now go to work…

~The General

How this impacted my day:

_____
_____
_____
_____
_____
_____

Tips from The General on the sales management part of the business...

Misquotations in sales are the only quotations that are never misquoted.

Got it? Now go to work...

~The General

How this impacted my day:

Tips from The General on the sales management part of the business...

The best thing to do behind an associate's back is to pat it.

Got it? Now go to work...

~The General

How this impacted my day:

_____
_____
_____
_____
_____
_____

Tips from The General on the sales management part of the business...

As a manager in sales, measure your success not by how much money you made this week or month, but by how much you developed the people who work for you this week or this month.

Got it? Now go to work...

~The General

How this impacted my day:

_____
_____
_____
_____
_____
_____

Tips from The General on the sales management part of the business...

The world's shortest class on being a first-class manager in sales:

1. *Know your people.*
2. *Know your stuff.*

Got it? Now go to work...

                    ~The General

How this impacted my day:

_____
_____
_____
_____
_____
_____

Tips from The General on the sales business...

I tell you and you forget.
I show you and you remember.
I involve you and you understand it.

Got it? Now go to work...

~The General

How this impacted my day:

Tips from The General on the sales management part of the business...

You can develop more salespeople in a month by being interested in them than in one year trying to get them interested in you.

Got it? Now go to work...

~The General

How this impacted my day:

_____
_____
_____
_____
_____
_____

Tips from The General on the sales management part of the business…

As a manager in sales, the best way to solve your own problems is to help your salespeople solve theirs.

Got it? Now go to work…

~The General

How this impacted my day:

Tips from The General on the sales management part of the business...

Good leaders know where they are always going in sales, but can also inspire along the way.

Got it? Now go to work...

~The General

How this impacted my day:

_____
_____
_____
_____
_____
_____

Tips from The General on the sales management part of the business…

Convince them that the only way you can grow together is to work together.

Got it? Now go to work…

~The General

How this impacted my day:

Tips from The General on the sales business…

After a great month, many heroes present themselves. Most of the time, it's not the ones you thought it would be. You can build on these people.

Got it? Now go to work…

~The General

How this impacted my day:

Tips from The General on the sales management part of the business...

Stop living on your past accomplishments. Your people are tired of you telling them how great you used to be. Go do something heroic this month with them. They will walk through fire after that with you.

Got it? Now go to work...

~The General

How this impacted my day:

Tips from The General on the sales management part of the business…

Bad months are temporary. Move on and get over it.

Good months are temporary also, but can be duplicated. Repeat what you did with your team or office this month with more enthusiasm and you will repeat. Then everyone will want your business card and your e-mail inbox will be filled.

Got it? Now go to work…

~The General

How this impacted my day:

_____
_____
_____
_____
_____
_____

Tips from The General on the sales management part of the business...

Everyone's favorite radio station...

WII FM *"What's in it for me?"*

People will go to great lengths for you provided there is something in it for them. They will buy, they will sell, they will look, they will refer, and they will help. We are wired this way unfortunately. Understand this and succeed with it.

Got it? Now go to work...

~The General

How this impacted my day:

Tips from The General on the sales management part of the business…

Character is doing what's right when nobody's looking.

J.C. Watts

Got it? Now go to work…

~The General

How this impacted my day:

Tips from The General on the sales management part of the business…

As a manager in sales, you have shown the ability to sell your product or service whenever you want to. That is the one confidence that you bring to the table everyday. Widen your confidence. Teach others what you have been taught.

Got it? Now go to work…

~The General

How this impacted my day:

Tips from The General on the sales management part of the business...

Help others get ahead. You will always stand out amongst your peers with that habit.

Got it? Now go to work...

~The General

How this impacted my day:

Tips from The General on the sales management part of the business...

There are spaces between your fingers so that another person's fingers can fill them. Go shake some hands today. Be a leader and show some product today.

Got it? Now go to work...

~The General

How this impacted my day:

Tips from The General on the sales management part of the business...

Never deprive someone of hope in sales. It might be all they have. Never forget when you first started.

Got it? Now go to work...

~The General

How this impacted my day:

_____
_____
_____
_____
_____
_____

Tips from The General on the sales management part of the business...

There is no greater feeling in sales management than making an impact on someone's life. Make them never forget you.

Got it? Now go to work...

~The General

How this impacted my day:

Tips from The General on the sales management part of the business...

Treat your associates or team like you would with the pictures of your family and loved ones. Put them in the best light.

Got it? Now go to work...

~The General

How this impacted my day:

_____
_____
_____
_____
_____
_____

Tips from The General on the sales management part of the business...

Ultimately, you are judged as a good leader by how good your people are. Can you make definite improvements there? Do it today.

Got it? Now go to work...

~The General

How this impacted my day:

Tips from The General on the sales business...

You take people as far as they will go in their career, not as far as you would like them to go.

Got it? Now go to work...

~The General

How this impacted my day:

_____
_____
_____
_____
_____
_____

Tips from The General on the sales management part of the business…

Poor time managers in sales almost always end up being poor money managers. If you're struggling with your money, it's almost always because you are struggling with your time.

Got it? Now go to work…

~The General

How this impacted my day:

_____
_____
_____
_____
_____
_____

Tips from The General on the sales management part of the business…

Only the mediocre salespeople are always at their best in sales. Have a meeting with them. Set some goals for them and then help them achieve them. They will forever be in debt to you, and you can call upon them the next time you need them.

By the way, you will need them one day.

Got it? Now go to work…

~The General

How this impacted my day:

Tips from The General on the sales management part of the business…

The worst thing that can happen is when one of your good people will not commit to moving forward in their sales career. This is where you come in. Inspire them and sell them to do it.

Got it? Now go to work…

                            ~The General

How this impacted my day:

Tips from The General on the sales management part of the business...

You will find that some people know how to sell your product or service great. They just don't know how to work. That's where you come in as their manager. This type of person is just a couple of decisions away from being one of your great ones.

Got it? Now go to work...

~The General

How this impacted my day:

_____
_____
_____
_____
_____
_____

Tips from The General on the sales management part of the business…

Everyone moves on in sales. The key is to control their exit.

Got it? Now go to work…

~The General

How this impacted my day:

Tips from The General on the sales management part of the business…

Don't sit at your desk today. Understand that if you are not on the street every now and then, you will forget what it's like on the street. Then your business slides. New and old need to see that you can still flex your muscles with the best of them.

Got it? Now go to work…

~The General

How this impacted my day:

_____
_____
_____
_____
_____
_____

Tips from The General on the sales management part of the business...

When recruiting, know this: Eagles never flock— you find them one at a time.

H. Ross Perot

Got it? Now go to work...

~The General

How this impacted my day:

Tips from The General on the sales management part of the business...

Do you think having enough sales or enough sales associates is enough? No, it is not! It's only enough. Never be happy with the amount of people you have.

Got it? Now go to work...

~The General

How this impacted my day:

_____
_____
_____
_____
_____
_____

Tips from The General on the sales business...

It's unfortunate. One-third are coming in, one-third are staying, and one-third are on their way out. As a manager, work on these stats.

Got it? Now go to work...

~The General

How this impacted my day:

Tips from The General on the sales business...

Those who say they don't need to be stroked a little every now and then, will lie to you about other things, too.

Got it? Now go to work...

~The General

How this impacted my day:

Tips from The General on the sales management part of the business…

Many want to fish, but few want to bring bait. Many people want to sell, but few want to help generate leads.

Got it? Now go to work…

~The General

How this impacted my day:

_____
_____
_____
_____
_____
_____

Tips from The General on the sales management part of the business...

Don't form judgments of salespeople from what other companies have told you about them.

Got it? Now go to work...

~The General

How this impacted my day:

_____
_____
_____
_____
_____
_____

Tips from The General on the sales management part of the business...

Eagles don't hunt mice. Go out and make a couple of thousand bucks this week.

Got it? Now go to work...

~The General

How this impacted my day:

Tips from The General on the sales management part of the business…

A street-smart manager does some of the dirty work himself, making sure his people know about it.

Got it? Now go to work…

~The General

How this impacted my day:

_____
_____
_____
_____
_____
_____

Tips from The General on the sales management part of the business…

When recruiting, always remember that intelligent people and educated people are not the same.

Got it? Now go to work…

~The General

How this impacted my day:

_____
_____
_____
_____
_____
_____

Tips from The General on the sales management part of the business...

Don't change your company's program to suit your needs or the needs of your people.

Got it? Now go to work...

~The General

How this impacted my day:

_____
_____
_____
_____
_____
_____

Tips from The General on the sales management part of the business...

Your people will do half of the great things that you do, and all of the things you shouldn't be doing.

Got it? Now go to work...

~The General

How this impacted my day:

Tips from The General on the sales management part of the business...

Can you look in the mirror every night and honestly say you did everything you could do to help you and your people succeed? If you can, start looking for a bigger house. If you can't, start looking for a good bankruptcy attorney.

Got it? Now go to work...

~The General

How this impacted my day:

_____

_____

_____

_____

_____

_____

Tips from The General on the sales management part of the business…

Nobody that you can build on wants to follow a small thinker. Get bigger in your thinking and you will energize your team immediately.

Got it? Now go to work…

~The General

How this impacted my day:

Tips from The General on the sales management part of the business…

Put your pen down and go shake ten people's hands this morning.

Got it? Now go to work…

~The General

How this impacted my day:

_____
_____
_____
_____
_____
_____

Tips from The General on the sales management part of the business…

Quit finding faults in your people as if you earn a promotion by it.

Got it? Now go to work…

~The General

How this impacted my day:

Tips from The General on the sales management part of the business…

The price of success costs you hard work. The price of failure will cost you everything.

Got it? Now go to work…

~The General

How this impacted my day:

Tips from The General on the sales management part of the business...

Good leaders know where they are going. They can also motivate and inspire their team to go with them. Go and inspire today.

Got it? Now go to work...

~The General

How this impacted my day:

Tips from The General on the sales management part of the business...

You have the ability to sell your product any time you want to. That is the one confidence that you bring to the table every day. Now is the time to widen that confidence and teach more people what you know.

Got it? Now go to work...

~The General

How this impacted my day:

_____
_____
_____
_____
_____
_____

Tips from The General on the sales management part of the business…

It's been said many times that leadership is about taking your people that you are responsible for, to a place where they would have never gone before without your presence or decision making.

Got it? Now go to work…

~The General

How this impacted my day:

Tips from The General on the sales management part of the business…

In matters of style, swim with the current. In matters of principle, stand like a rock.

Thomas Jefferson

Got it? Now go to work…

~The General

How this impacted my day:

_____

_____

_____

_____

_____

_____

Tips from The General on the sales management part of the business…

Help others get ahead. You always stand taller with others on your shoulders.

Got it? Now go to work…

~The General

How this impacted my day:

_____
_____
_____
_____
_____
_____

Tips from The General on the sales management part of the business…

I use not only all the brains I have, but all the brains I can borrow.

Woodrow Wilson

Got it? Now go to work…

~The General

How this impacted my day:

_____
_____
_____
_____
_____
_____

Tips from The General on the sales management part of the business...

Daddy Rhino said to his baby Rhino:
"You need to develop thick skin if you are to make it here in the jungle."

Develop some "thick-skinned" salespeople.
Successful salespeople hear more "no's" in one day, than most people hear in one month. They have to have thick skin for this.

Got it? Now go to work...

~The General

How this impacted my day:

_____
_____
_____
_____
_____
_____

Tips from The General on the sales business…

A seven-course meal is not a six-pack and a hot dog. If you're going to do this business the right way, you not only have to take care of your head but your body, too. Eat right when you can and take some vitamins. You're no good to anyone when you're less than 100%.

Got it? Now go to work…

~The General

How this impacted my day:

_____
_____
_____
_____
_____
_____

Tips from The General on the sales management part of the business…

If one of your salespeople tells you they are ready to quit, convince them to at least sell one more before they quit. You will keep them forever and both of you will be happy.

Got it? Now go to work…

~The General

How this impacted my day:

_____

_____

_____

_____

_____

_____

Tips from The General on the sales management part of the business...

Being a good manager is a 24/7 job. Understand that they will call you with problems all the time. You signed on for it, so deal with it or delegate it.

Got it? Now go to work...

~The General

How this impacted my day:

Tips from The General on the sales management part of the business…

No matter how many "good salespeople" you think you have, there is always room for one more. Go find and develop one this month.

Got it? Now go to work…

~The General

How this impacted my day:

Tips from The General on the sales management part of the business…

Never put your salespeople before your family. Family will always be there. Most salespeople come and go. Never forget this.

Got it? Now go to work…

~The General

How this impacted my day:

_____
_____
_____
_____
_____
_____

Tips from The General on the sales management part of the business…

Give people second chances. It is difficult, but many times they turn out to be your highest performers. They remember you gave them another chance.

Got it? Now go to work…

~The General

How this impacted my day:

_____
_____
_____
_____
_____
_____

Tips from The General on the sales management part of the business...

Reading what people "doodle" about during meetings often informs you on what is going on in their lives. Many times, it also means you need to work with the person giving the meeting.

Got it? Now go to work...

> *~The General*

How this impacted my day:

_____
_____
_____
_____
_____
_____

Tips from The General on the sales management part of the business...

Music is great to listen to but your car is a university on wheels if you listen to the right things about sales and management. You can earn the equivalent of a college degree if you use your time wisely.

Got it? Now go to work...

~The General

How this impacted my day:

_____
_____
_____
_____
_____
_____

Tips from The General on the sales management part of the business...

Sometimes a salesperson who starts out real slow turns out to be awesome. You were probably that person when you look back on your start.

Got it? Now go to work...

~The General

How this impacted my day:

Tips from The General in the sales management part of the business...

Watch out for "parrots" in this business. All talk and can't fly. Don't get too sold on these people. They just waste everyone's time.

Got it? Now go to work...

~The General

How this impacted my day:

_____

_____

_____

_____

_____

_____

Tips from The General on the sales management part of the business…

You should always listen to the old salespeople every now and then. They are like living history books and can still teach you a thing or two.

Got it? Now go to work…

~The General

How this impacted my day:

Tips from The General on the sales management part of the business...

Never make a decision unless you are willing to live up to the consequences.

Got it? Now go to work...

~The General

How this impacted my day:

_____
_____
_____
_____
_____
_____

Tips from The General on the sales management part of the business…

The real art of sales management is not what you hear from your salesperson's mouth, but what you see in their heart and their eyes.

Got it? Now go to work…

~The General

How this impacted my day:

_____

_____

_____

_____

_____

_____

Tips from The General on the sales management part of the business...

Sometimes the best answer to your salesperson's request is just no. Learn to say no. You will have more money and a happier relationship with your spouse at home.

Got it? Now go to work...

~The General

How this impacted my day:

Tips from The General on the sales management part of the business…

In middle management, the truth is the quickest and easiest way out of trouble.

Got it? Now go to work…

~The General

How this impacted my day:

_____
_____
_____
_____
_____
_____

Tips from The General on the sales management part of the business...

Be careful around the new people just recruited into the business. It is surprising how much impact a word or gesture can make on them.

Got it? Now go to work...

~The General

How this impacted my day:

_____
_____
_____
_____
_____
_____

Tips from The General on the sales management part of the business…

Don't look for a lot of compliments at this level. It's your job to give them to the people who deserve them now.

Got it? Now go to work…

~The General

How this impacted my day:

_____

_____

_____

_____

_____

_____

Tips from The General on the sales management part of the business...

Small gestures of thoughtfulness and kindness can mean a lot—I mean a whole lot to some people who work for you. Work on this more and you will see increases in production from these people.

Got it? Now go to work...

~The General

How this impacted my day:

_____
_____
_____
_____
_____
_____

Tips from The General on the sales management part of the business…

When the spouse of your salesperson is happy at home, your salesperson will perform great at work. Adjust this to the specific needs of your people. Cards and phone calls go a long way when their spouse is out working late at night.

Got it? Now go to work…

~The General

How this impacted my day:

_____

_____

_____

_____

_____

_____

Tips from The General on the sales management part of the business…

Get a little crazy and do things out of the ordinary in your meetings and day today. It is always rewarding for your people to see you are different.

Got it? Now go to work…

~The General

How this impacted my day:

_____
_____
_____
_____
_____
_____

Tips from The General on the sales management part of the business…

I watched my best friend, David Kayne, make millions in the sales business. His secret is quite simple.

"Prosperity through Promotion"

Got it? Now go to work…

~The General

How this impacted my day:

Final tip from The General…

Why were there 212 tips in this book?
Go to tip number 77 and see for yourself.

Got it? Now go to work…

~The General

The General would love to hear from you!

Write to him or send him an e-mail and let him know how the book inspired you. Don't be surprised when he writes back to you.

For additional copies, please call, write, or fax to the address listed below. For your convenience, fill out the order form below and fax or mail it to The General's office.

The General
The Estates at Ivy Creek
2745 Ivy Hill Drive
Buford, Georgia 30519

Fax: *770.271.4998*

E-mail: thegeneralsells@yahoo.com
On the web at: www.thegeneralsells.com/

Hello General!

_____Enclosed is my story on my recent success for you to share and enjoy with others!

_____Please contact me about information on quantity discounts on your book!

_____Please send me _____ more book(s). Please contact me at _____ to get my shipping address and payment information.

I would like The General to come motivate, educate and
stimulate my group.
Please contact me at _____
My name is _____
My company is _____
We are located in _____
Our product/service is _____

GENERAL (jen - er al)—Having extended
command, holding the highest rank of persons
affecting a particular group.

ANTIDOTE (an/ti - dote)—A remedy for counteracting
the effects of poison, disease, etc. Something that prevents
unwanted effects. (negative attitude etc.)

The General

About The General:

The General is a door-to-door salesman—a real one. His best friend gave him the name sometime ago. He started his career in direct sales at age nineteen selling vacuum cleaners door to door on commission. He rose through the ranks quickly and found himself a champion recruiter and trainer. He went on the road sharing his knowledge of sales, motivating thousands of men and women, teaching them that they, too, with just average backgrounds and a strong desire can become champions in sales.

Still in his twenties, he opened his own franchise selling vacuum cleaners and quickly found himself one of the top in his district and soon after tops in the state, and eventually in the top 10 percent worldwide. The General won several sales contests including trips all over the world, expensive jewelry, and luxury automobiles. He opened more than twenty locations during his time as a franchise owner.

The following bits of information in the form of antidotes, quirks, and quips he picked up on the road or experienced them himself in his twenty-five years of door-to-door sales and managing people. Some of them he thought of himself; others he gladly gave credit to. The rest? He does not remember where they came from, so he will just pass them on to you as they were passed onto him.

Today, his consulting company helps companies with recruiting, training and motivation. Everyday is a battle in sales. Ours is still the greatest business for the average person to get a job and hold their head up. Let The General be your daily coach. There are 212 pieces of advice. Simply read each page, apply what you have learned, and then write down how it impacted your day. Commit yourself to greatness and follow through. Watch your ATTITUDE, PERFORMANCE and INCOME go up!

Enjoy!

Printed in the United States
89318LV00004B/88-141/A